Mike and Hilary Wreford's

OKEHAMPT

COLLECTION

A. E. REED
15 STATION ROAD
OKEHAMPTON, DEVON
EX20 1DY (0837) 52841

To Alfie
Best wishes
Hilary & Mike

OBELISK PUBLICATIONS

Other Books in this Series

Thanks to the Express & Echo, Exeter for permission to reproduce the photos on pages 26 and 29.

For further details of these or any of our extensive Devon titles, please contact us at 2 Church Hill, Pinhoe, Exeter, EX4 9ER, Tel: (0392) 468556.

ISBN: 0 946651 72 8

Other Obelisk Publications

First Published in 1993 by Obelisk Publications
2 Church Hill, Pinhoe, Exeter, Devon
Designed by Chips and Sally Barber
Typeset by Sally Barber
Printed in Great Britain by
Sprint Print Co Ltd, Okehampton Place, Exeter

This Fore Street photograph shows the two rival jewellers W.H. Cornish and E. Stinchcombe in adjoining shops. They had a mutual respect for each other and only disagreed over religion. W. Cornish was a pillar of the Church of England, whilst E. Stinchcombe was a strong non-conformist, and who served the community well as a captain of the Boys' Brigade. Next to Cornish's is Blackmore's, then the popular baker's 'Marks' and, of course, Meechams Temperance Hotel.

The posters in Cornish's windows indicate they were having a closing down sale before moving to 7 Fore Street, opposite the Arcade. W. Cornish is now, with over 100 years' service, the longest established family business in the town.

The person on the extreme right with the straw hat is Mr Lugg who was responsible for so many photographs of the town and inhabitants, and for many moorland paintings. A truly talented man.

The coronation of King George VI was the justifiable reason for this tea party, in Fore Street on 12 May 1937. The loyalty and patriotism of the Okehampton inhabitants were much in evidence, judging by the crowds, the numerous flags and bunting. This photograph and the one on the adjoining page were both used in a Westcountry TV Quiz show "Westwise" for the Okehampton team to identify – unfortunately they didn't! Despite the bypass, present day traffic would make this type of event in Fore Street nigh impossible. The long established Plume of Feathers is in the foreground; we're sure they did a roaring trade that day!

One of the biggest Street Parties ever held in Okehampton was for the arrival of the railway in 1871. The Okehampton Railway Company was set up in 1862. The line from Coleford Junction reached North Tawton in 1865 and Sampford Courtenay in 1867 (having become the Devon and Cornwall Railway en route). For four more years passengers from Okehampton were carted hazardously up and down Appledore Hill in wagonettes. When the connection was finally complete in October 1871, the town celebrated a new era of advanced communications.

Shown here at the end of the 1914/18 war, is grandfather George Clinnick at the entrance of his cobbler's shop on the corner of Northfield/Crediton Road. He was a respected shoemaker of the day making his 'Meldon Boots' at 7 shillings and 6 pence (37½p) with unconditional 12 months guarantee. These were much in demand by the quarrymen and other workers.

The housing difficulties of that period can be appreciated by the fact that this 3-bedroomed house, not only accommodated him and his wife, but daughter, son-in-law and grandchildren Will, Charles, May, Maggie, Barbara and his sister Charlotte.

The shop subsequently changed to Ogdens, and then became Williams Fish and Chip shop. Happily today this shop continues to serve the public as a greengrocer's run by June and Stuart Shobbrook, following in their father's footsteps.

Mrs Matilda Cornish is pictured standing between her entrepreneurial sons. Both Jack and Jim were butchers but the coincidence is that they occupied adjacent corner shops in Northfield Road. On her right is Jim who was the proprietor of No. 29. Jack (Claude Cockwill's father) is on her left and ran the butcher's shop on the other side of the 'Drang' at No. 31.

Like so many shopkeepers at the time, Jack supplemented his income by a country round, and was a popular figure in the Sourton area. The New Inn, now 'The Highwayman', was his best customer judging by the length of time his pony and trap could be seen outside!

This imposing house situated at the beginning of Castle Road was the Horne family home. It included a guest house, and tea gardens with delicious produce from the neighbouring Dartmoor Dairy. Bought by the GPO, it was demolished in 1938 to create a site for the new Post Office. It was subsequently commandeered as a coal yard by the Army during the war.

The Okehampton Borough Council had considered it as a site for the new Town Hall, but this did not come to fruition. However 1962 saw the completion of the new crown post office and telephone exchange in Okehampton.

Here is a 1930 staff photograph of the Okehampton and District Co-operative Society Ltd taken outside the shop on the corner of Kempley Road / St James Street. The van delivery driver is Lewis (Tich) Lobb who had to drive to Tavistock early every morning to collect the fresh bread for the day; although afterwards they baked their own. His largest customer was the Okehampton Artillery Camp, and this was a regular morning delivery. The tall figure in the doorway is Fred Dalton the Manager, with popular Bill Pike on his left. Bill Pike, of course, left to run his Crediton Road shop for many years, a real 'open all hours' establishment.

The Butcher's to the left was Westlake's which today continues as A.L. Martin and Son Ltd.

9

OPENING CEREMONY.

BRIGADIER-GENERAL DONALD INSPECTING THE TROOPS.

The opening of the Drill Hall on 1 July 1914 for the military and social uses of the local company of the 6th Devon Regiment, was the occasion of a joint military and civic demonstration and some celebration in Okehampton.

Here Brigadier-General C.G. Donald commanding the Wessex Division is received in Fore Street by a guard of honour from the 6th Devon's, which he duly inspected. There followed a public luncheon in the Market Hall, with the official opening in the afternoon.

The Drill Hall is now the home of Okehampton Conservative Club, and members may be surprised to know that the cost of the building was a princely £2,250.

Watkins the Butcher is at the back separating West Street and Rosemary Row. These premises were subsequently occupied by the Midland Bank and then Dartmoor Dairy before being demolished for widening.

Tuesday evening of 1 October 1940 saw bombs falling in Okehampton. This picture shows indomitable baker W. (Bill) Hutchings carrying on business on the pavement outside his West Street premises damaged during the raid.

His happy notice 'Business As Usual – Keep Smiling' says it all!

The market cattle pens were extensively damaged during the raid – one 10-foot iron bar was hurled over a row of houses 100 yards away. Although four people were injured, the only recorded fatality was a blackbird!

When the Lord Mayor of London, Sir William Treloar, with one of his Sheriffs, Sir William H. Dunn, arrived at Okehampton Station, they were welcomed by the Mayor, civic leaders, and a large crowd of onlookers.

General Holley, who was to accommodate the guests during their stay in Okehampton, arrived with two cars to convey the party to Oaklands. This scene shows General Holley standing beside the driver; Sydney Simmons is on the left back with Sir William Treloar.

Incidentally, such was the importance attached to the visit, that the London and South Western Railway Co insisted their divisional superintendent Mr G.F. Vallance travelled with the train from Exeter to Okehampton.

The opening ceremony of Simmons Park was performed at 3.00 p.m. on Monday, 8 July 1907, by the Lord Mayor of London, the Right Honourable Sir William Purdie Treloar. A grandstand was erected at the park entrance near the Masonic Lodge; this provided protection from the incessant rain for the visiting dignitaries.

Judging by the chains of office, it was probably the largest number of Devonshire mayors ever assembled in Okehampton. The proud Mayor of Okehampton was the local prominent businessman Mr William Bird German.

THE SIMMONS CASKET,

On the unique occasion when Okehampton was given the park, the public proceedings started with the presentation of the freedom of the borough to Sydney Simmons and to the Lord Mayor.

Although shown as the 'Simmons Casket' in the above photograph, there were actually two identical caskets that contained certificates when presented to the two freemen. The caskets were of silver gilt, having enamel pictures of the castle and park entrance on one side and on the other an inscription recording the date of the presentation. Surmounting the caskets, as can be seen, is the Borough coat of arms. The cost of the caskets was £11 each and, to ensure fair trading, the Borough Council purchased one each from E. Stinchcombe and W.H. Cornish.

14

Simmons Park, Okehampton

Sydney Simmons is standing in the foreground with chalet 'Treloar' clearly visible behind him. Nearby is the showpiece rustic bridge spanning the artificial ponds, which have provided Okehampton children so much fun over the years. This wooden structure was removed in the summer of 1913 and replaced by one of concrete. The craftsman was Mr W.J. Paltridge a local mason of New Road. The bridge cost £8.3s.10d, which included materials and ten days' labour at the princely sum of 5 shillings per day.

In the early part of the century, the Paltridge family included a large number of traders, including carpenters, shoemaker, school teachers, straw hat maker and of course three blacksmiths as befits the time. There is still a bridge there today.

This is a 1925 photograph of the Okehampton Picture Palace that opened in 1915. The cinema was built by Blatchford and Dawe, adapting premises previously occupied by Cornish's the drapers.

This photograph left to right shows G. Robinson resplendent in his commissionaire's uniform, who doubled as a chimney sweep during the day. Also in the picture is Alice Medland, Frank Petherick (sitting, projectionist), boy usher – unknown, Mrs Williams, Miss Higgins (pianist), Reg Cullington (chocolate boy – nicknamed 'Buttons'). Sally Holmes who was the next pianist became known as 'the bird of paradise'. It was initially leased to an Exeter Cinema firm (Peters) who owned a cinema blitzed during the war, then subsequently owned by Simeon Newcombe. The name was changed to 'the Premier' with the advent of talking pictures. As the television network spread, business declined and it became a supermarket, then a night-club, where its tradition for entertainment continues under the name of Nero's.

With the arrival of the railway the bottom of Station Road became very popular for shops. Yellands on the right was a poulterer, also advertising Devonshire clotted cream. These premises then became the Okehampton branch of the 'West Devon Electric Supply Co Ltd' subsequently the South Western Electricity Board in 1948. We assume therefore the gas lamp was soon changed to electric!? Next is the stationer's shop of well-known Okehampton Councillor and businessman Charlie Sprague – a man of multi-talents. A.R. Bray lived in the next house, with his draper's shop the adjoining property. This shop subsequently passed to a Mr Harris of Holsworthy, before becoming in turn 'The Labour Club', Wippels, the library and is now a printing shop. As can be seen, Station Road was unsurfaced at the time, so the council 'mud scraper' was necessary in winter but was also used for spraying water to dampen the dust in summer!

Devon Motor Transport (DMT) was delighted to demonstrate its new fleet of twenty-seater Thorneycroft coaches in 1925. It was quite a day when the coaches and crews paraded at Kempleys Meadow (now the pleasure grounds). Station Road is very noticeable in the background, although of course today with the growth of trees the houses are less evident. DMT was formed initially as a freight carrying company after 1918, with the registered offices in Old West Street, and the workshops and garages in the George Hotel Yard (now Jacobs Pool).

From September 1923 DMT expanded by buying existing companies and opening up routes throughout Devon and Cornwall. However, after being taken over themselves the depot closed in 1930 and this enterprise which at one time employed 200 people came to a sad end.

With such a large work force DMT formed a Sports and Social Club, with a soccer team in the old West Devon Football League. Okehampton Ivyleaves were in the same league and fans were able to enjoy some friendly derby matches.

This photograph was to celebrate their league championship of 1926/27.

Although not featured in this photograph, their most celebrated player was former Plymouth Argyle favourite 'Daisy Bell'. He was part of their forward line – known as the 'busy bees' as each name began with the letter 'B'!

Back L to R: Jack Cockwill, Jack Knight, Jack Lovell, Bert Northcott, Ray Tancock, Fred Hill. Standing: Unknown, unknown, Ern Northcott, unknown, Phillips (goalkeeper), Happy Down, Harold Lappage, Charlie Box, unknown, Sparky Lang. Sitting: George Mallett, Les Yeo, Charlie Trollope, Percy Mugridge (Capt), Dick Northcott (Manager), Percy Knight, Sam Wreford.

Known as the Mansion House, and later Old Mansion Courts, when it was used as flats, this was an imposing building in East Street, almost opposite Pipers Court.

With the entrance protruding into East Street, and the building deteriorating, the difficult decision was taken to demolish. All the stones were removed to the council yard, after being numbered, then stored, with the intention to rebuild to its former glory, but in another location. Unfortunately this did not come to fruition and the stones have long since disappeared!

Pictured here, in 1927, is the Mayor, Mr Percy Edgecombe, posing proudly for the camera with the new 'Borough of Okehampton' fire engine. This replaced the old horse-drawn four-in-hand appliance. This fire engine had no windscreen, solid tyres, and had to be hand started. There were only brakes on the back wheels that were four inches wide. Back row (L to R) Seth Allen, Bill Gillard, Alan Brunskill (Borough Surveyor), Joe Howard, George Gale, Reg Horne. Standing: Walter Collacott, Bill Ellis, Bill Hain (Capt), Mr Edgecombe (Mayor), Ted Bubear, George Knott. The three-storey building in the background was G. U. Fulford's store before being burnt down during a blizzard in the 1950s!

The new Wesleyan Chapel is pictured here not long after the official opening on 1 March 1904, a day much appreciated by Wesleyans of Okehampton Town and District.

The cost of the complete building was approximately £4,200 of which £3,700 was raised before the chapel was finished. It was much helped by the 52 allocated foundation stones on which a minimum sum of £10 each had been laid and this realised £831. Alderman Rowse, the Mayor, attended, and it was pleasing to note the entire Corporation supported him, regardless of their religious denominations.

To conserve water the Okehampton Borough Council used to 'turn off' water supplies during the night.

The popular figure of 'Dozy Weeks' was very familiar with Okehampton townsfolk as he performed this task twice a day at the bottom of Station Road. He earned his nickname as he would not move for any mode of transport, expecting them to navigate around him.

A large chain driven vehicle was loaded with girders at the station, designed for the construction of Friars Hele railway bridge. Whilst descending Station Road, the chain broke and the brakes failed; in the resulting chaos in Fairplace, the immovable 'Dozy' was killed.

This is a 1930 picture of the staff of T. Day & Sons Ltd taken outside their Ford showroom/service department in New Road. These premises were beside the West Ockment River and with the Old Wesleyan Chapel and workshops opposite, provided large facilities for a staff that numbered over forty. The firm had started as a cycle shop in the arcade, developing into one of the pioneers of the motor engineering trade in the area.

An additional responsibility was the operation of the ambulance, under initially the Okehampton Motor Ambulance committee and later the St John Ambulance. Such disquiet was raised at one time that occasionally an injured person was collected by 'two motor mechanics' without first aid training. Nevertheless the staff of T. Day and Sons Ltd provided this service over the years with distinction.

Every town, village and even hamlet enjoyed the skilled services of the local blacksmith. Okehampton had several, but this one pictured above is the west end forge in New Road. This building remains almost unchanged by the passing years, with Mr Sam Ball being the proprietor before moving to Bridestowe. Afterwards it ran successfully with George Gale, who had moved from North Street after working with 'Granfer' Lovell. The wheelwright's stone can be seen in the foreground.

Okehampton Argyle – Devon Junior Cup Winners 1946/47 – are pictured here at St James' Park, Exeter after beating Astor Institute 4-0. This was probably the strongest side in the history of the football club, all the players being capable of playing to the standard of league football. Denzil Mortimer for instance, as a young schoolmaster, had played as an amateur for Exeter City before the war. He subsequently had a successful trial for Arsenal, but the outbreak of war prevented what would have been a successful career with the London club.

After the war Denzil contributed much both academically and to sport with the Okehampton Secondary Modern School, before being appointed Head of North Tawton. He then became Head of the Lower School when Okehampton became comprehensive.

Eric Furse created a record of forty playing years with the club before retiring aged 55 years. (L to R): Denzil Mortimer, George Crews, Eddie Guy, Ron Connor, Eric Furse (Capt on shoulders) Dave Hearn, Denis Guy, Bill Stewart, Jack Roberts, Bill Jarvis, Maurice Sage.

Like the Football club, the Okehampton 'Columbines' Women's Hockey club was very strong after the war. Two of the players in the Okehampton Devon County Tournament winning side of 1950 were the wives of footballers; when not supporting their husbands, Janie Mortimer and Joy Crews could be seen demonstrating their skills on the hockey field. All round sportswoman Marjorie Measures skippered the side for many years, having already captained the British Universities XI. Marjorie was soon a regular member of the county side and went on to become a selector for the Devon and Western territory sides. Mary Eccles, Fuzzie Phillips and Janie Mortimer also achieved county recognition. Back row (L to R): Judith McNeil, Joan Pauley, Patsy Gratton, Marjorie Measures (Capt), Peggy Brooking (Umpire), Ducarol Stewart, Joy Crews. Kneeling front row: Lavinia Parker, Vera Northcott, Mary Eccles, Fuzzie Phillips, Janie Mortimer.

Both rugby teams are featured in 1931 when Okehampton played host to the Devon Barbarians. The picture was taken behind the stand at Cowlings Field (now Saville Mead). The Devon Barbarians were made up of players from major clubs in the county, and played midweek against some of the leading club sides.

On the left, standing between the referee and county captain, E.G. Butcher, is the unmistakable figure of Derek Brown, who later served as a Lieutenant Colonel in the Territorial Army during the war. He was prominent as a solicitor in Okehampton and HM Coroner for the area. At the same time he contributed much to the sporting life, politics and Royal British Legion of Okehampton and the county of Devon. In the centre wearing the trilby, is club president and builder W.J. Avery. The front row sitting down comprises: Ossie Parker, Dick Hawkin, Norman Lowe, Buz Palmer.

The Okehampton Cricket first team is shown here, ready to play Alphington in the first game of the 1953 season. Back row: Mike Booth, 'Robbie' Roberts, Ken Westcott, Brian Gaywood, 'Sgt' Baker, Jeff Wooldridge, Mike Wreford. Front row: Rev. Neville Sutton, David Tucker (Capt), Fred Duffy, George Crews. Farmer David Tucker was the ever-popular skipper and star batsman for many years after the war. He scored countless runs and centuries for the club and showed outstanding leadership as captain. Fred Duffy, David Tucker and Mike Wreford are all now life members of the club.

Okehampton residents were delighted when Sydney Simmons consented to open the new 9-hole golf course on 16 July 1913. Mr Simmons was an ardent golfer and although living in North Finchley was still the largest shareholder in the newly formed company. This course was laid by the great open champion J.H. Taylor and when it was extended to 18 holes in 1923 it was opened by two ex-open champions J.H. Taylor and Alex Heard.

Such was the immediate impact of the course that one visitor at the time, after a good round and a good lunch, was heard to exclaim, "If heaven is anything like as good as this, I don't mind going there." Perhaps this was a reflection on the actual height of this moorland course!

It was the Dartmoor guide James Perrott who started the pilgrimages to Cranmere Pool, but there can seldom have been a more distinguished group visiting than this! Pictured here during his 1921 tour of the Duchy, is Edward, Prince of Wales, later King Edward VIII before his abdication. With him (left to right) are Sir Walter Peacock, Admiral Sir Lionel Halsey, Mr William Proudfoot, Lord Clinton, Mr Jim Endacott and Mr Ralegh Phillpotts. The only other member of this party was the intrepid Western Morning News *photographer, to whom the heir apparent observed, "You deserve fifty photographs for carrying this ten miles," as he tested the weight of the camera.*

31

The Dartmoor Dairy was established in Okehampton for many years. The father and son team of Sydney and Reg Horne participated in every carnival for well over 25 years. The two oxen's heads were considered to be from the last two working oxen in the Okehampton area, afterwards given to the R.A.O.B. The dairy business was popular with the locals and holidaymakers. The military however contributed greatly to their 'cream by post' business, as the soldiers wanted to send a taste of the west country home to their loved ones! This 1910 trade entry features left to right: Syd Horne (on horseback), Miss Baker, Mr Glass (Lady), Reg Horne (Girl) and C. Bolt.

The 1921 carnival again featured Sydney and Reg Horne, this time outside James Wright & Co, Ironmongers, (and a good many other things besides). Ever keen to contribute to charity and the carnival, they ran a competition selling milk at 3d a quart, which each purchaser had to guess where the milk ran out! The lucky winner received a free supply of milk for a week. The Kings Arms can be seen in the background. Sid and Reg Horne ran the Dartmoor Dairy and often during the summer they would dispatch one hundredweight of cream in their 'cream by post' business in just one day!

It was almost by accident that Meldon Quarry was established. It came as a result of the construction of the railway line two to three miles west of Okehampton. The rock was found to be very hard and impeding progress of the line, being about 1874. The Dartmoor stone was found to be very durable and therefore most suitable for ballast on the track. Soon stone was being used farther afield and the above photograph, taken around 1875, shows a section of the workforce. One can appreciate the hard physical work entailed. Horses of course were used extensively for many years. The quarry was officially established in 1897 but had been providing work for years. So, for well over 100 years it has been a major source of employment in the area with, at one time, 300 men working there.

Lynden Weaver, the popular quarry manager for 31 years, recalls that Italian prisoners of war were road building there in 1943, under the unusual presence of armed guards!

Meldon Viaduct is an imposing sight as it sits astride the West Ockment. The slender iron construction is an immense height, and originally built as a single track with single supports. However, this was thought to be unreliable and the size was increased to accommodate a second track with the supports augmented accordingly.

The lime kilns, on the left, are noticeable, and this was a busy and profitable moorland industry. Meldon Valley was found to be rich in minerals, and a valuable vein of granulite was discovered around 1880. For a time it was successfully used in glass making, comparing favourably with that of Dresden. It was Charles Geen who leased the quarry plus the lime quarries, which provided some useful employment, but it was not to last.

The War Department, investigating the possibility of using Dartmoor for artillery practice, responded to a suggestion from the Okehampton town council of the day and visited the northern edge. It found the area just above Okehampton ideal for the purpose and it was probably in August 1875 that the first camp originated. To this day the established camp is used for training in tough conditions anticipated when on active service. This is among our favourite photographs of the military on Dartmoor. It shows the vast number of men and horses undertaking manoeuvres with the Royal Field Artillery in a scene that resembles a 'John Wayne' film.

Times are changing, the year is 1926 and the horse soldier can be seen casting a watchful eye. However, motorised transport is beginning to replace the horse. The army was experimenting with all forms of transport and these Fordson tractors were being used with treads fitted to the wheels. These were eventually changed to 'caterpillar operation', which was far more suitable for rough terrain. The town has always had a good relationship with the army, the traders especially welcoming the extra business, with, no doubt, the town hostelries benefiting most!

The opening of the Okehampton and District Agricultural Show was always very much a 'state occasion' with more formality than there is today. Pictured here, just after the official opening of the 1896 'exhibition', is the mayor, accompanied by his mace bearers and the corporation.

Simon Peter Brendon Newcombe was mayor in 1894, 1895 and 1896 and played an important part in the civic and business life of the town. To those in need he was a welcoming figure, offering warming soup at his home, Fair View (now Kent House), in George Street.

Okehampton, East Street.

Taken in 1905, this picture shows a group of bandsmen who assembled for practice outside the Exeter Inn (now the Exeter Arms) in East Street. They were known as the 'thirsty-eight' because of their propensity to perform outside all the pubs in town. It was not, as legend suggests, that they had a drink in every pub, but that the revellers were much more generous in their donations to the band as they left! Formed by their conductor James (Barber) Coombe in 1892, this band delighted townsfolk with their renderings for ten years.

After returning from the Crimean war in 1856, this ardent musician contributed much, in many ways to the town, until his death in 1907 aged 83 years. It seems inconceivable, at a time when travelling was almost solely by horseback, that he once taught no less than seven bands, namely Okehampton, Sticklepath, South Zeal, North Tawton, Bow, Crediton and Witheridge.

Okehampton Parish Church.

The parish church of All Saints, Okehampton was consecrated to the service of God on 31 July 1261 although there is evidence that it was endowed in 1229. It was partly rebuilt in 1417, but it is generally not known that all but the tower was destroyed in the disastrous fire of 1842. It is a tribute to the people of the time that the foundation stone of the new church was laid in November 1842 and the church re-opened on the 11 April 1844. Amongst the gravestones in the churchyard are those with inscriptions to the French prisoners of war who died here in 1811–1815.

Agnes Baden-Powell, who developed the Girl Guides, would have been proud of this Okehampton company shown at Simmons Park in 1920. Under their captain Miss Spearpoint (standing far right), this photograph contains many guides who practised 'good and happy citizenship' throughout their lives, often at difficult times. Although we have been unable to identify all the guides, this picture includes Ethel Wotton, May Orchard, Louise Jewell, Rose Seymour, Gwen Bowdridge, Mildred Weaver, Lil Farley, Ivy Pedrick, Rose Palmer, Edna Lias, Florrie Seymour, Lily Lowe, Joan Wright, Lily Earland, Ethel Yeo, Beattie Yeo and Monica Wright. The guides would meet every Friday in the Old Church Room in North Street.

Mrs Cynthia Foskett of Okehampton, soon after her arrest on a charge of impersonating Queen Victoria. A vaulting horse, diving-suit, inner-tube, Arapahoe head-dress, eight pairs of manacles and a pound of sprouts were taken into police custody, but the ferret succeeded in escaping.

This photograph has always interested us although we have never been able to trace Cynthia Foskett. However it is obvious she must have caused a stir at the time, although of course it might have been some satirical comment from a publication of the day?

This council meeting in December 1929 took place on the occasion of J.J. Newcombe completing 25 years as town clerk; the opportunity was taken to present him with a silver salver. At the same time, the mayor, Alderman W.B. Chammings received the freedom of the Borough. J.J. Newcombe went on to complete over 50 years as town clerk, but if that is thought to be exceptional, earlier Solon Luxmore completed 55 years in the same position. Back: S. Newcombe, P. Edgecombe, W.B. Chammings (Mayor), S. Horne, A.W. Coles. Front: A.E. Worden, C. Bray, C. Sprague, J.J. Newcombe (town clerk), R.A. Brunskill (Borough Surveyor), G.U. Fulford, C. Smale and a council clerk.

Turning back the clock is really fascinating. This picturesque scene (circa 1775–1800) shows Painter's Court/Sparrows Court – now the site of the Carlton Cinema. Although clean and neatly kept inside, the two Courts had to be demolished under the slum clearance scheme of Okehampton Borough Council. This was at a time when government regulations encouraged 'new for old'!

This lead to the council's housing development in North Road. The Carlton Cinema was erected on this site but not without opposition from Mr S. Newcombe who could command an audience of 300 at the Premier Cinema. Representing Mr Newcombe, Mr A.W. Fullwood argued the case in the Okehampton Sessions on 12 August 1936. However the bench approved the plan and the Carlton was built at a cost of some £8,000. Both cinemas ran in tandem for many years, until the closure of the Premier.

It was on 'Bluebell Sunday' in May 1917 that the castle was presented to the town, together with £1,000 in consuls for its upkeep. Mr Hawkins was the caretaker at the time. Sadly the Castle Lodge, seen here, has been demolished. The castle grounds were the venue for this Okehampton Primary School tea party of 1912.

Sydney Simmons had purchased the castle in 1911. He spent a considerable sum of money on restoration and other work, as he wished the grounds to become 'a veritable Garden of Eden' for all to enjoy. The work was completed in May 1912 and the Primary School was one of the first to view the finished work. Sydney Simmons was keen for all organisations to make full use of the castle and grounds for academic and social purposes. To this day, entry to the castle is free on 'Bluebell Sunday'.

Fitz's Well, Okehampton.

Fitz's Well, situated near the military camp, has been the subject of many tales throughout the centuries. It is identified by the ancient cross and may derive its name from the family of John Fitz who acquired the manor of Meldon around 1585. An old superstition is that if you are lost on Dartmoor, take a drink from the well and your deliverance will be assured. There is a thought that this cross was removed from a position at Halstock Chapel by 'many horsemen'!

Okehampton

In this early view from the station, perhaps the only familiar sight is of the cricket match, which has not changed with the passage of time. The large college complex of today now occupies a major part of the fields and the pleasure grounds have been formed. Over the years, buildings such as the sports hall, squash courts, cricket pavilion, sports pavilion and swimming pool have been added, alongside the tennis, bowling and putting facilities, for the enjoyment of all. Altogether a jewel in Okehampton's crown!

The most magnificent building in Okehampton is 'Oaklands', formerly known as 'Sweetlands'. It was built by Albany Saville in the early part of the 19th century. He was appointed MP for Okehampton in 1807, serving with distinction until his resignation in 1820. On 17 June 1818, the two elected MPs for Okehampton were Albany and his brother Christopher but this partnership was not to last as Christopher died after less than a year's service. The Saville family served the community well and was always associated with every much needed charitable institution within the Borough. Oaklands became the home of the Holley family – first James Hunt Holley then his eldest son, Wyndham Hunt. On his death in 1898, the estate was inherited by his brother the famous General Holley. At today's values, it seems inconceivable that this house, together with 94 acres, was sold to George Gratton in 1930, for the princely sum of £5,100!